W9-AQI-936

Saginaw Chippewa Tribal College
2274 Enterprise Drive
WITHDRAWN
Mt. Pleasant, MI 48858

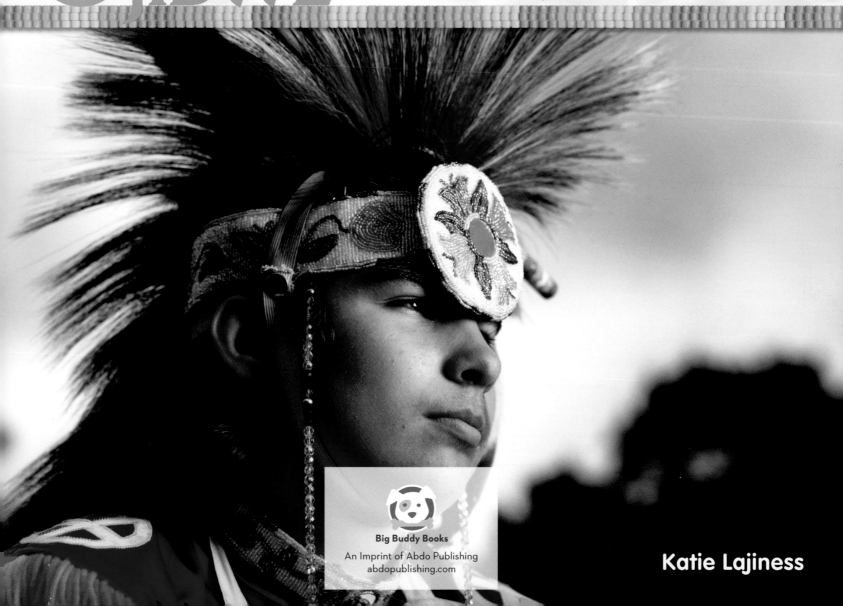

OJIBWE

Big Buddy Books
An Imprint of Abdo Publishing
abdopublishing.com

Katie Lajiness

abdopublishing.com

Published by Abdo Publishing, a division of ABDO, PO Box 398166, Minneapolis, Minnesota 55439.
Copyright © 2019 by Abdo Consulting Group, Inc. International copyrights reserved in all countries. No part
of this book may be reproduced in any form without written permission from the publisher. Big Buddy Books™
is a trademark and logo of Abdo Publishing.

Printed in the United States of America, North Mankato, Minnesota.
052018
092018

THIS BOOK CONTAINS
RECYCLED MATERIALS

Cover Photo: Dan Callister/Alamy Stock Photo.
Background Photo: Gail Shotlander/Getty Images.
Interior Photos: Elfstrom/Getty Images (p. 17); Florilegius/Alamy Stock Photo (p. 23); Glen Stubbe/AP Images
    (p. 27); John Brueske/Getty Images (p. 25); Katelyn Downs Photography/Getty Images (p. 19); Keith Crowley/
    Alamy Stock Photo (p. 5); Marilyn Angel Wynn/Native Stock (pp. 9, 11, 13, 15, 16, 17); Mark Bridger/Getty
    Images (p. 30); Photawa/Getty Images (p. 21); Science History Images/Alamy Stock Photo (p. 26); Stacey
    Newman/Getty Images (p. 29).

Coordinating Series Editor: Tamara L. Britton
Contributing Editor: Jill Roesler
Graphic Design: Jenny Christensen, Maria Hosley

Library of Congress Control Number: 2017962686

Publisher's Cataloging-in-Publication Data

Name: Lajiness, Katie, author.
Title: Ojibwe / by Katie Lajiness.
Description: Minneapolis, Minnesota : Abdo Publishing, 2019. | Series: Native Americans
    set 4 | Includes online resources and index.
Identifiers: ISBN 9781532115103 (lib.bdg.) | ISBN 9781532155826 (ebook)
Subjects: LCSH: Ojibwa Indians--Juvenile literature. | Indians of North America--Juvenile
    literature. | Indigenous peoples--Social life and customs--Juvenile literature. |
    Cultural anthropology--Juvenile literature.
Classification: DDC 970.00497--dc23

CONTENTS

AMAZING PEOPLE

Hundreds of years ago, North America was mostly wild, open land. Native American tribes lived on the land. Each had its own language and **customs**.

The Ojibwe (Oh-jihb-WAY) are one Native American tribe. Many know them for their **ceremonies** and handmade crafts. Let's learn more about these Native Americans.

Did You Know?

The Ojibwe call themselves *Anishinaabe* (ah-nish-NA-bay). This means "the people."

Early French settlers called the Ojibwe Saulteurs (SOO-tuhrs). The Canadian province Saskatchewan is named for the tribe.

5

Ojibwe Territory

   The Ojibwe are one of North America's largest tribes. Their homelands were in what is now Saskatchewan, Manitoba, Ontario, and Quebec in Canada. In the United States, the tribe also lived in present-day North Dakota, Minnesota, Wisconsin, and Michigan.

CANADA

UNITED STATES

MEXICO

OJIBWE HOMELANDS

SASKATCHEWAN

MANITOBA

ONTARIO

QUEBEC

NORTH
DAKOTA

MINNESOTA

WISCONSIN

MICHIGAN

Home Life

The Ojibwe were **nomadic** people. As animal herds traveled, the Ojibwe had to quickly take down their wigwams and move.

To set up their homes, women tied trees into a dome-shaped frame. In the summer, they covered it with birch bark, cattails, and reeds. During the winter, they covered the wigwams with animal furs.

A large wigwam held several families and had two campfires.

What They Ate

The Ojibwe gathered wild rice in the fall. They brushed the rice into their boats with long sticks. Then they roasted it and stored it for winter.

In warm weather, men fished from birchbark canoes. And in the winter, they fished through holes cut into ice-covered lakes.

The Ojibwe also hunted ducks, geese, and rabbits. And they planted sweet potatoes, pumpkins, corn, beans, and squash.

Sometimes Ojibwe men hunted elk, deer, or moose.

11

Daily Life

Tribe members made deerskin clothes. Women stripped plant stems and used the dried matter to make fabric.

Women wore dresses and men wore loincloths. Everyone had leggings and moccasins. In winter, people added buckskin robes or used blankets as coats.

Women used porcupine quills to sew seed beads onto clothes.

13

Ojibwe men and women had different jobs. Women prepared most of the food and made the clothes. Men fought in war, hunted, and fished. Together, Ojibwe tapped maple trees for sap they made into sugar. They also gathered wild rice in their canoes.

Ojibwe men built small canoes for their children to play with.

MADE BY HAND

The Ojibwe made many objects by hand. They often used natural supplies. These arts and crafts added beauty to everyday life.

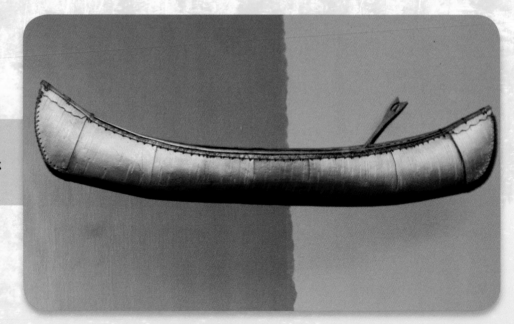

Birchbark Canoes
Ojibwe used birch bark to cover their canoes.

Beaded bags
Ojibwe women showed off their beadwork by sewing shoulder bags.

Snowshoes
Snowshoes were made from bent wood frames with leather webbing. These helped people walk on top of deep snow.

Cradleboards
Babies stayed warm inside cradleboards. Mothers tucked moss inside the bottom to keep the babies dry.

17

SPIRIT LIFE

Dreams are an important part of Ojibwe **culture**. Boys and girls learned to seek **visions** and dreams. Ojibwe believed dreams helped them connect to the spirit world. Sometimes, Ojibwe did not eat for days to gain knowledge about the universe. They believed this was the way to meet with their guiding spirits.

The Ojibwe hung handmade dream catchers to make sure they only had good dreams.

19

STORYTELLERS

Like many tribes, the Ojibwe have a creation story. Long ago, water covered the entire earth. Nanabozho (na-nuh-BOH-zoh) and his animal friends floated through the water on a boat. They each swam underwater for sand. But they failed.

Then Muskrat swam down and came back with sand in his paws. The winds blew until the ball of sand grew into what is now the earth.

Agawa Rock on Lake Superior features some early Ojibwe paintings. These paintings were made to tell stories of dreams, visions, and events.

Fighting for Land

Throughout history, the Ojibwe had to fight for their rights. Over hundreds of years, the Ojibwe lost land to European settlers. The tribe signed many **treaties** to protect their land and people. But broken promises left the Ojibwe with little food, shelter, or land.

In 1891, Ojibwe children were forced to attend **boarding schools**. There, teachers corrected them if they spoke their native language.

Ojibwe danced to tell stories about battles.

THE WAR DANCE, BY THE OJIBBEWAY INDIANS.

In the early 1900s, the government forced the Ojibwe to move onto **reservations**. Then in the 1950s, many Ojibwe had to move off reservations and into big cities.

But the Ojibwe wanted to keep their **culture**. Beginning in 1984, new reservations began in Michigan. In 1999, the Ojibwe won the right to hunt and fish on their old land.

The western side of Lake Mille Lacs is part of the Ojibwe reservation in Minnesota.

BACK IN TIME

900

Ancestors of the Ojibwe lived along the East Coast. They began to move toward the Midwest.

1400

Ancestors of the Ojibwe arrived in the Midwest.

1545

The Ojibwe spread throughout Wisconsin and Minnesota.

1754 to 1763

Tribe members joined the French to fight the British in the **French and Indian War**.

1850

More than 150 Ojibwe died from hunger and illness during the Big Sandy Lake **tragedy**.

1902

The US government sold land on the Mille Lacs **Reservation**. The Ojibwe had to move to the White Earth Reservation.

2008

The Oshki Manidoo Center was set up in Bemidji, Minnesota. It was a place to help Ojibwe with health problems.

1989

Ojibwe leader Winona LaDuke formed the White Earth Land Recovery Project. The group worked to take back the land the Ojibwe had lost.

2016

Minnesota Governor Mark Dayton announced that Columbus Day would become **Indigenous** Peoples' Day.

THE OJIBWE TODAY

The Ojibwe have a long, rich history. Many remember them for gathering wild rice and tapping maple syrup.

Ojibwe roots run deep. Today, the people have held on to those special things that make them Ojibwe. Even though times have changed, many people carry the **customs**, stories, and memories of the past into the present.

Did You Know?

Today, almost 200,000 Ojibwe live in North America.

Ojibwe continue to wear cultural clothes to share their history with others.

"The deer is my companion; I follow his life. I never need a compass to go through the woods, for I am able to find my way just like a deer."

— L'Anse, Ojibwe

GLOSSARY

ancestor a family member from an earlier time.

boarding school a school at which most of the students live during the school year.

ceremony a formal event on a special occasion.

culture (KUHL-chuhr) the arts, beliefs, and ways of life of a group of people.

custom a practice that has been around a long time and is common to a group or a place.

French and Indian War the war between France and Great Britain from 1754 to 1763.

indigenous produced, growing, living, or occurring naturally in a particular region or environment.

nomadic of or relating to people that travel from place to place.

reservation (reh-zuhr-VAY-shuhn) a piece of land set aside by the government for Native Americans to live on.

tragedy a disastrous event.

treaty an agreement made between two or more groups.

vision something dreamed or imagined.

Online Resources

Booklinks
NONFICTION NETWORK
FREE! ONLINE NONFICTION RESOURCES

To learn more about the Ojibwe, visit **abdobooklinks.com**. These links are routinely monitored and updated to provide the most current information available.

Index